HYMNS MADE EASY FOR VIOLA

With Guitar and Suggested Chordal Accompaniment

GENE CLARKE

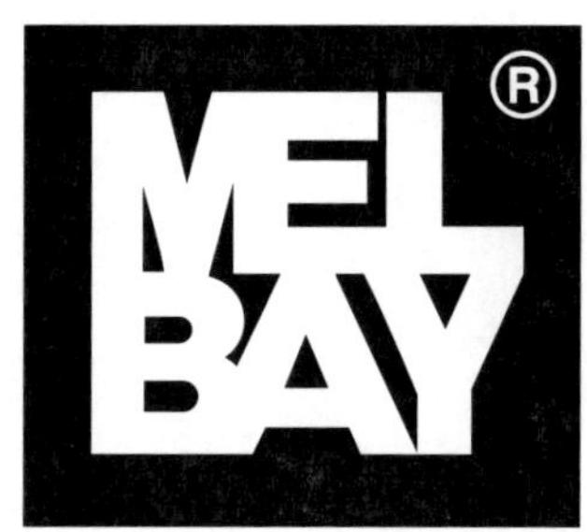

WWW.MELBAY.COM

Foreword

Hymns Made Easy for Viola is a collection of favorite traditional hymns with chordal accompaniment that can be used for church, for supplementary lesson material, or for recreational playing. All of the viola parts are in first position with bowing indicated, and chord names are printed above each staff. A guitar or any chordal instrument may play the chordal accompaniment. All of the arrangements in this book can be played together with the same titles in *Hymns Made Easy for Violin* and *Hymns Made Easy for Cello.*

Gene Clarke

Index of Hymns

Title	*Page*

Abide with Me

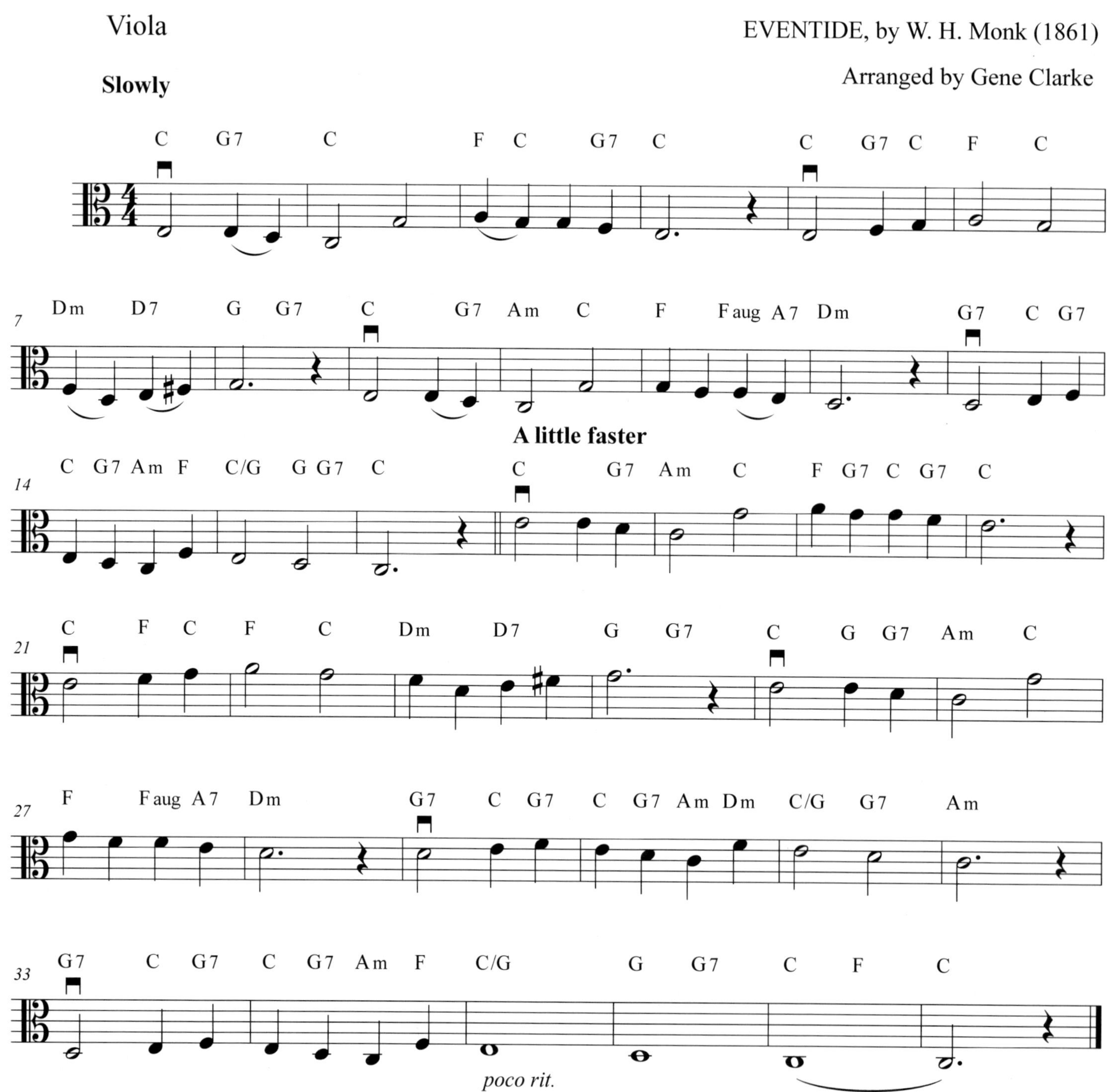

Alas! and Did My Savior Bleed?

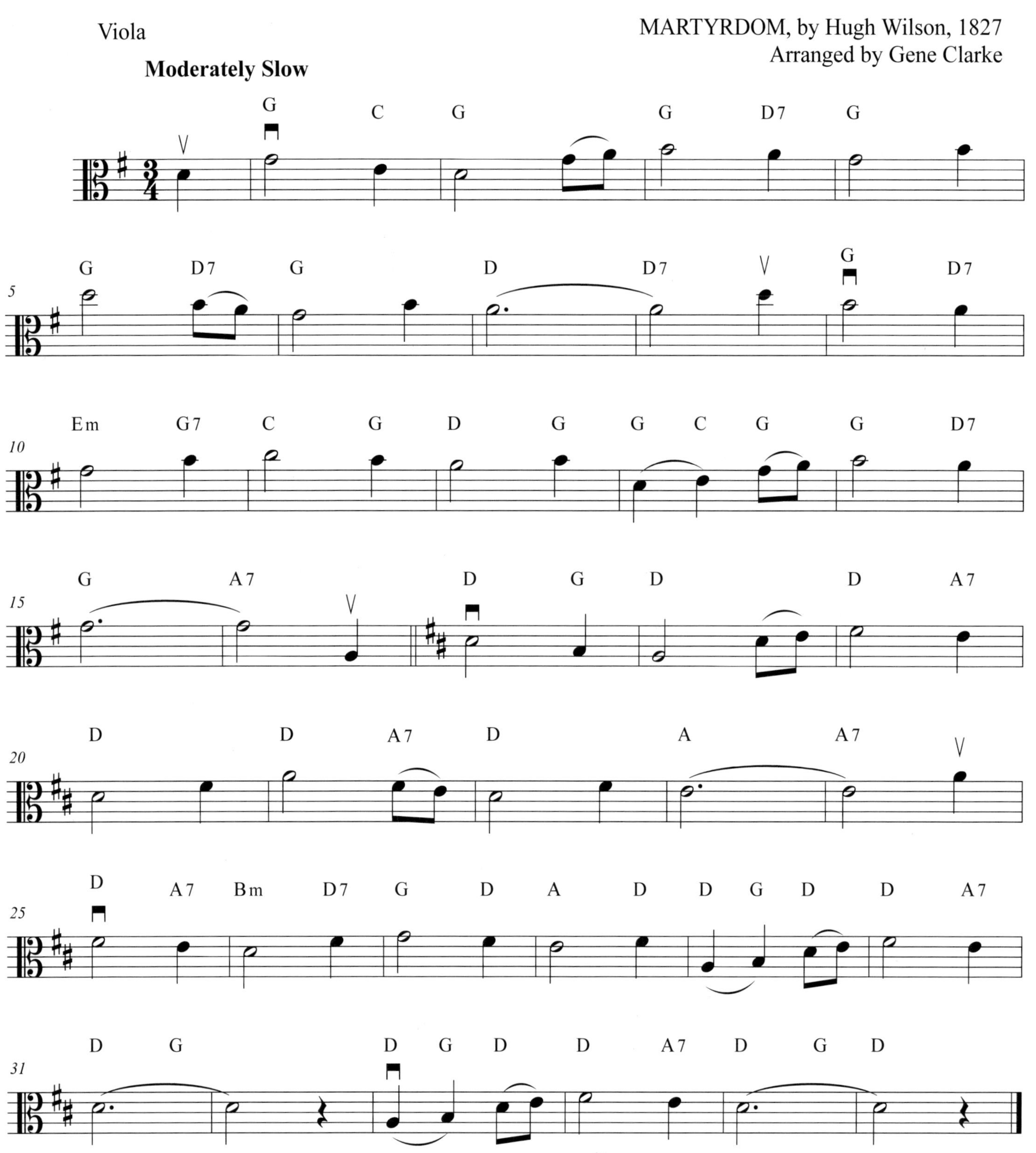

Am I a Soldier of the Cross?

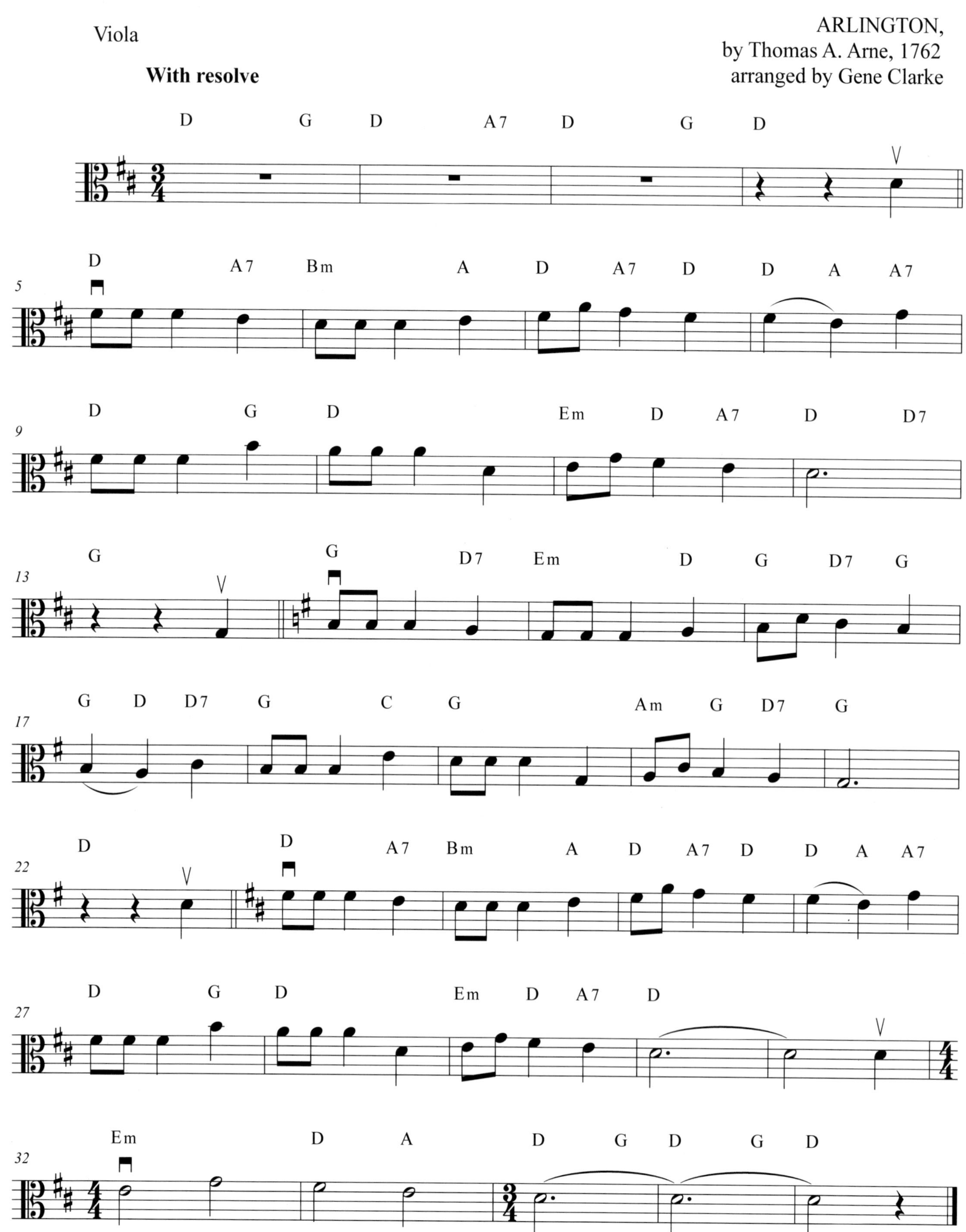

Amazing Grace

NEW BRITAIN,
19th Century American melody

Arranged by Gene Clarke

Viola

Moderately fast

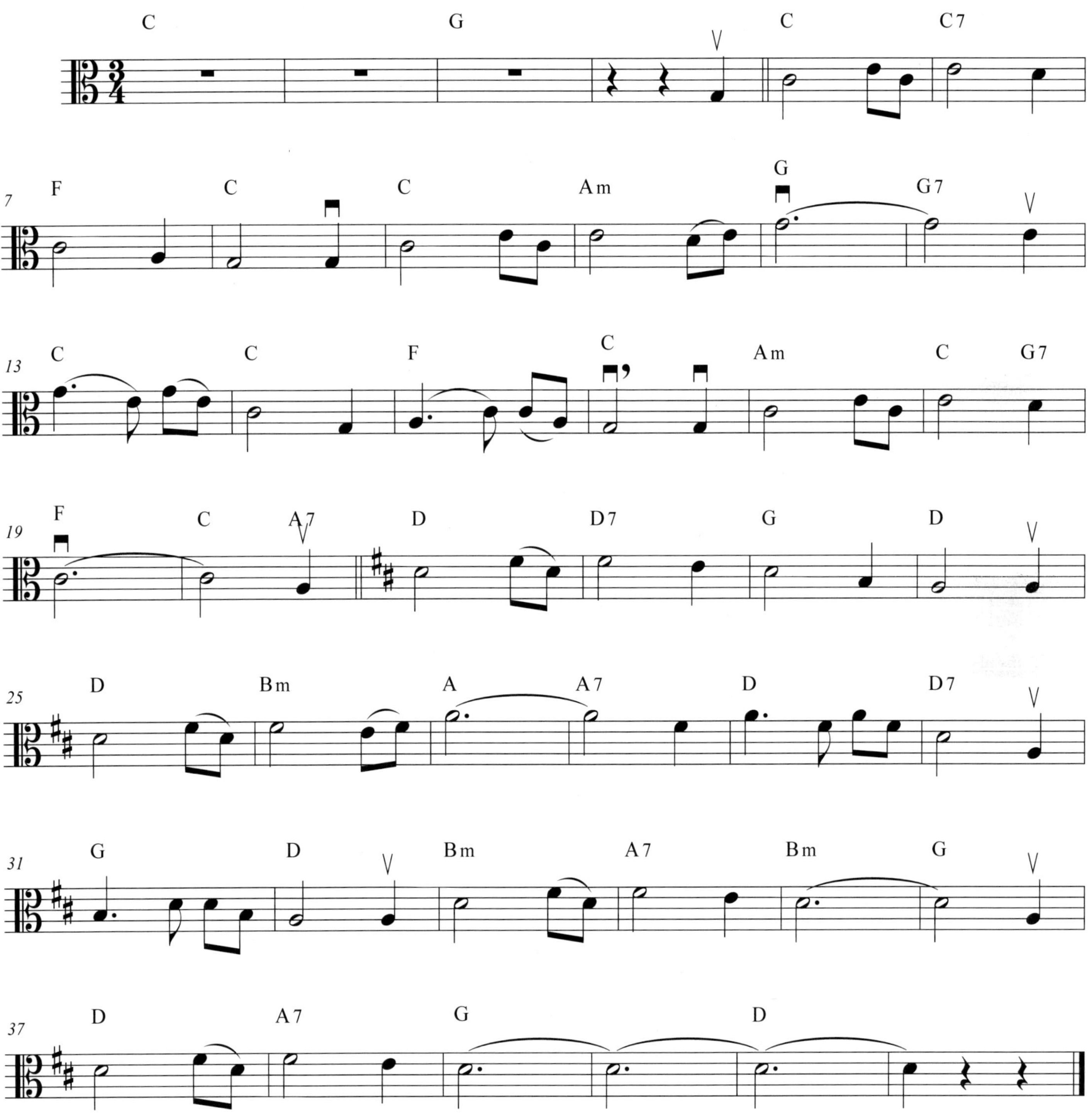

Ask Ye What Great Thing I Know

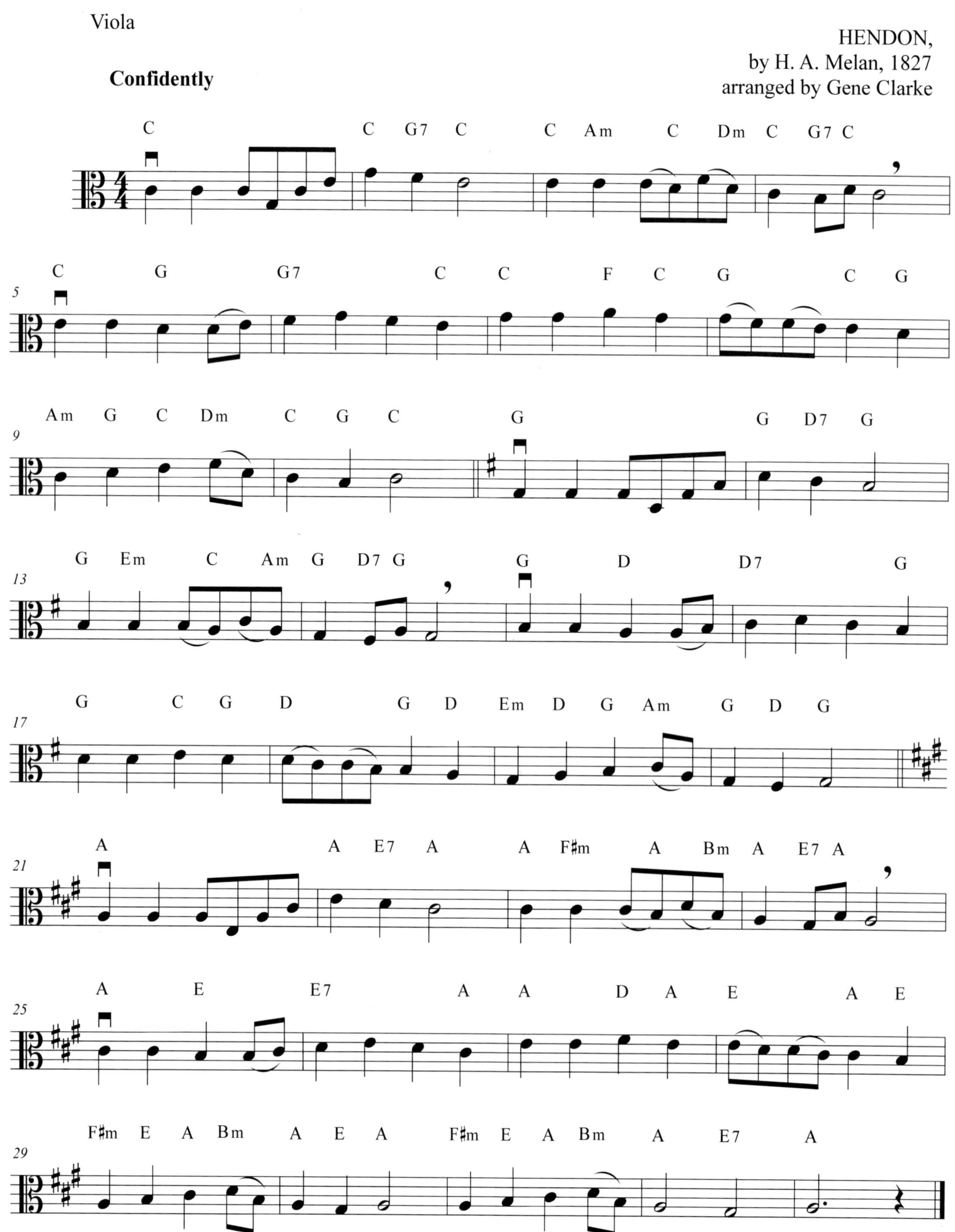

Blessed Assurance

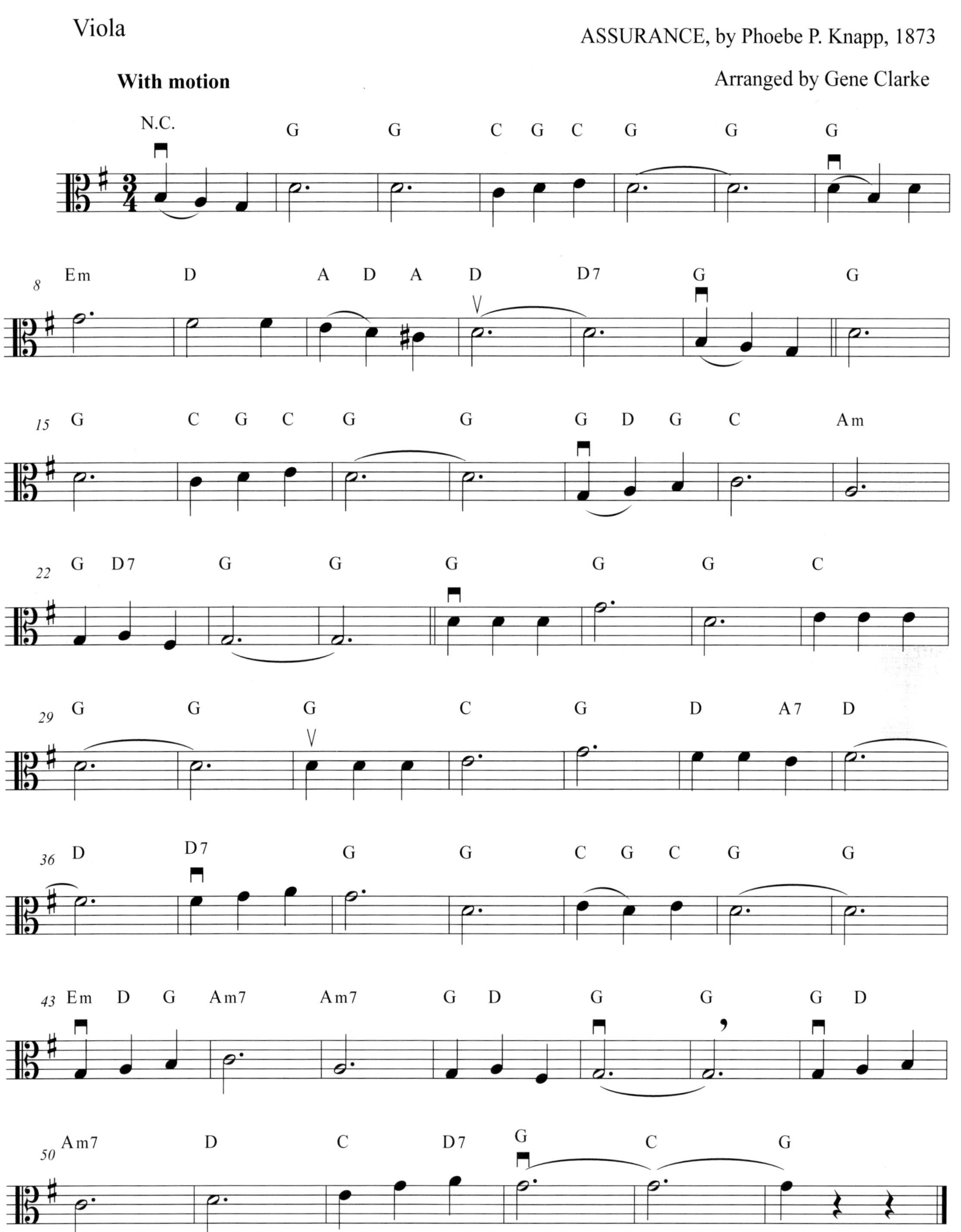

Blest Be the Tie that Binds

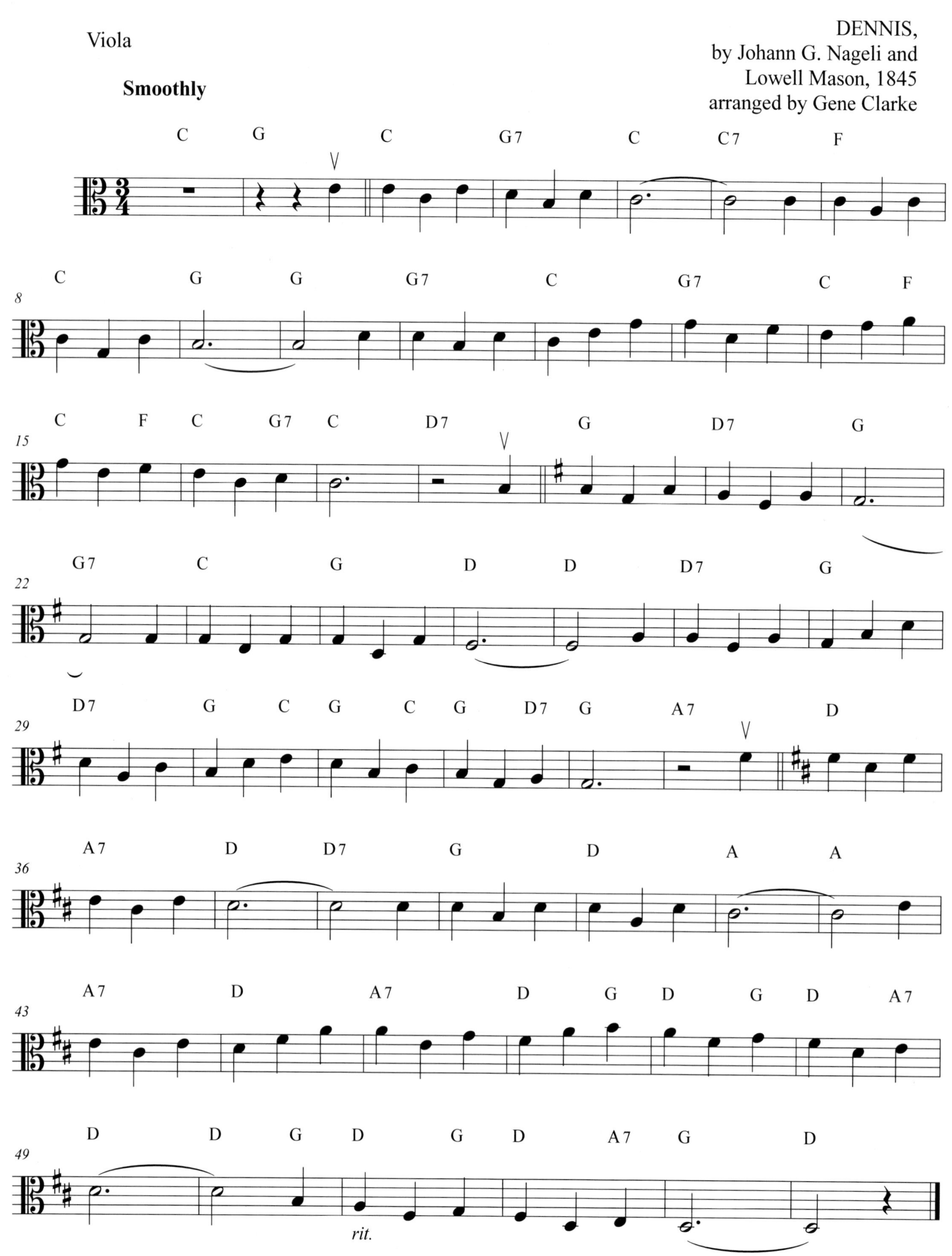

Break Thou the Bread of Life

Viola

BREAD OF LIFE,
by William F. Sherwin, 1877
arranged by Gene Clarke

With Reverence

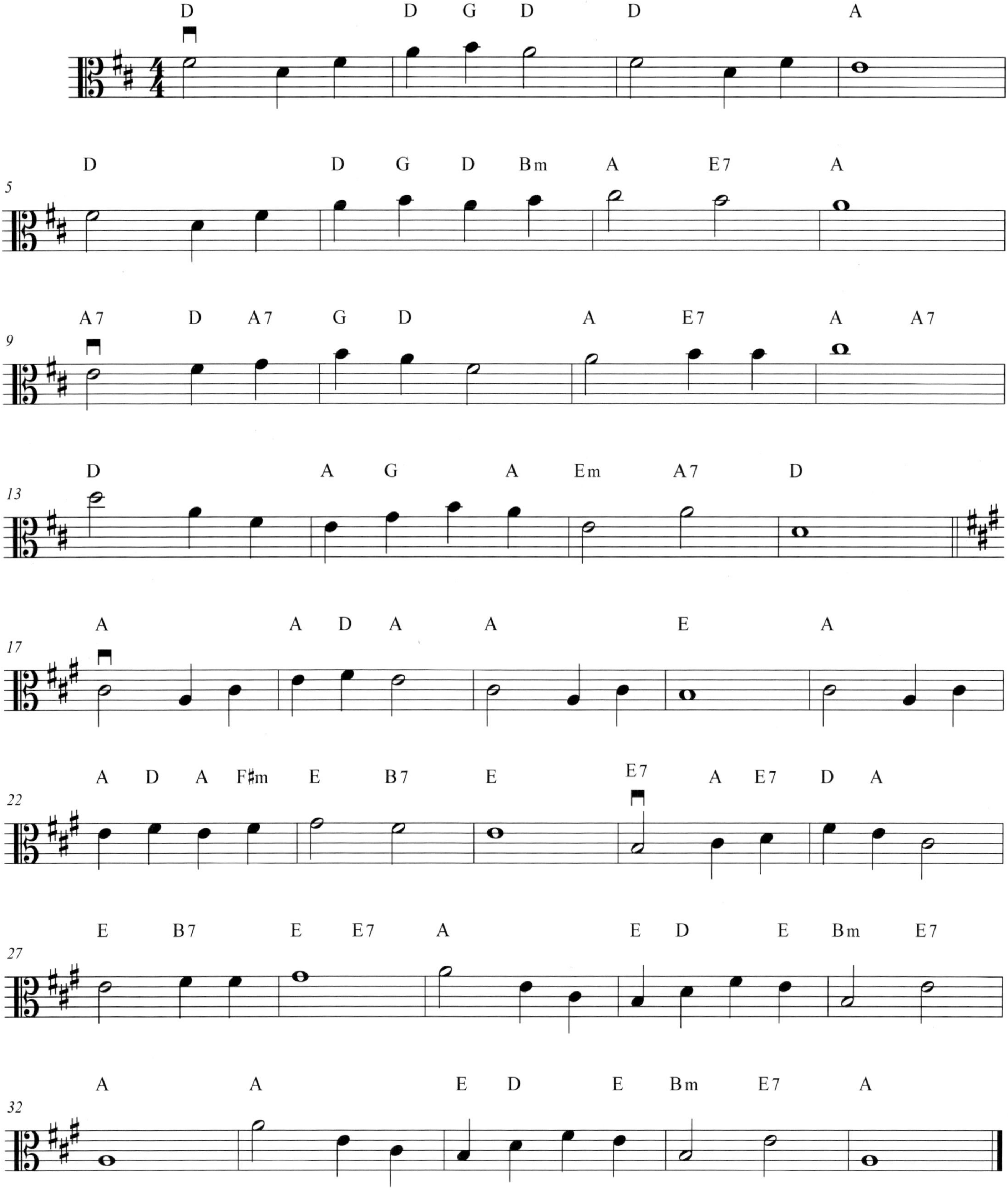

D D G D D A

D D G D Bm A E7 A

A7 D A7 G D A E7 A A7

D A G A Em A7 D

A A D A A E A

A D A F♯m E B7 E E7 A E7 D A

E B7 E E7 A E D E Bm E7

A A E D E Bm E7 A

Have Thine Own Way, Lord

Viola

ADELAIDE,
by George C. Stebbins, 1907
arranged by Gene Clarke

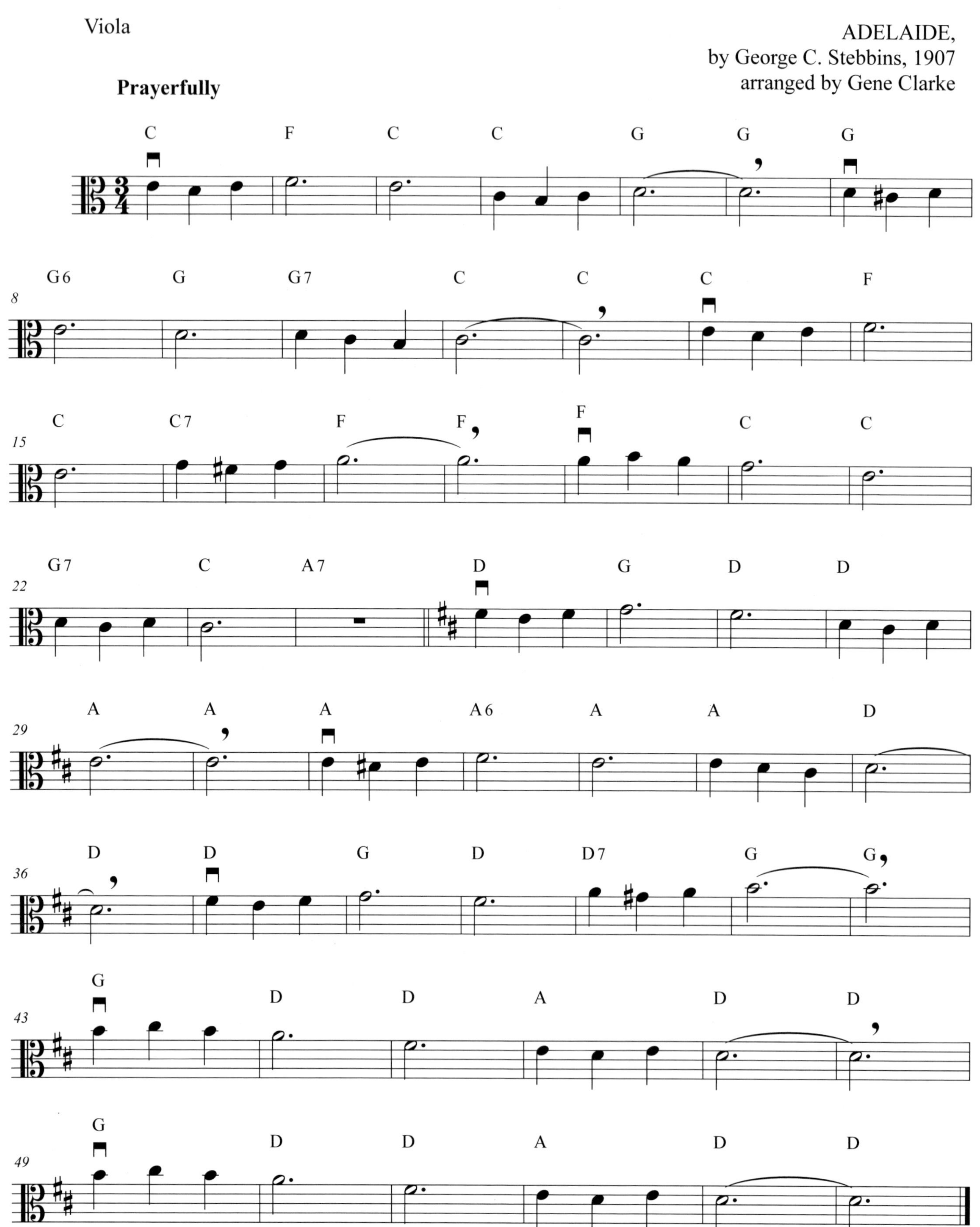

How Firm a Foundation

FOUNDATION, early American melody

Arranged by Gene Clarke

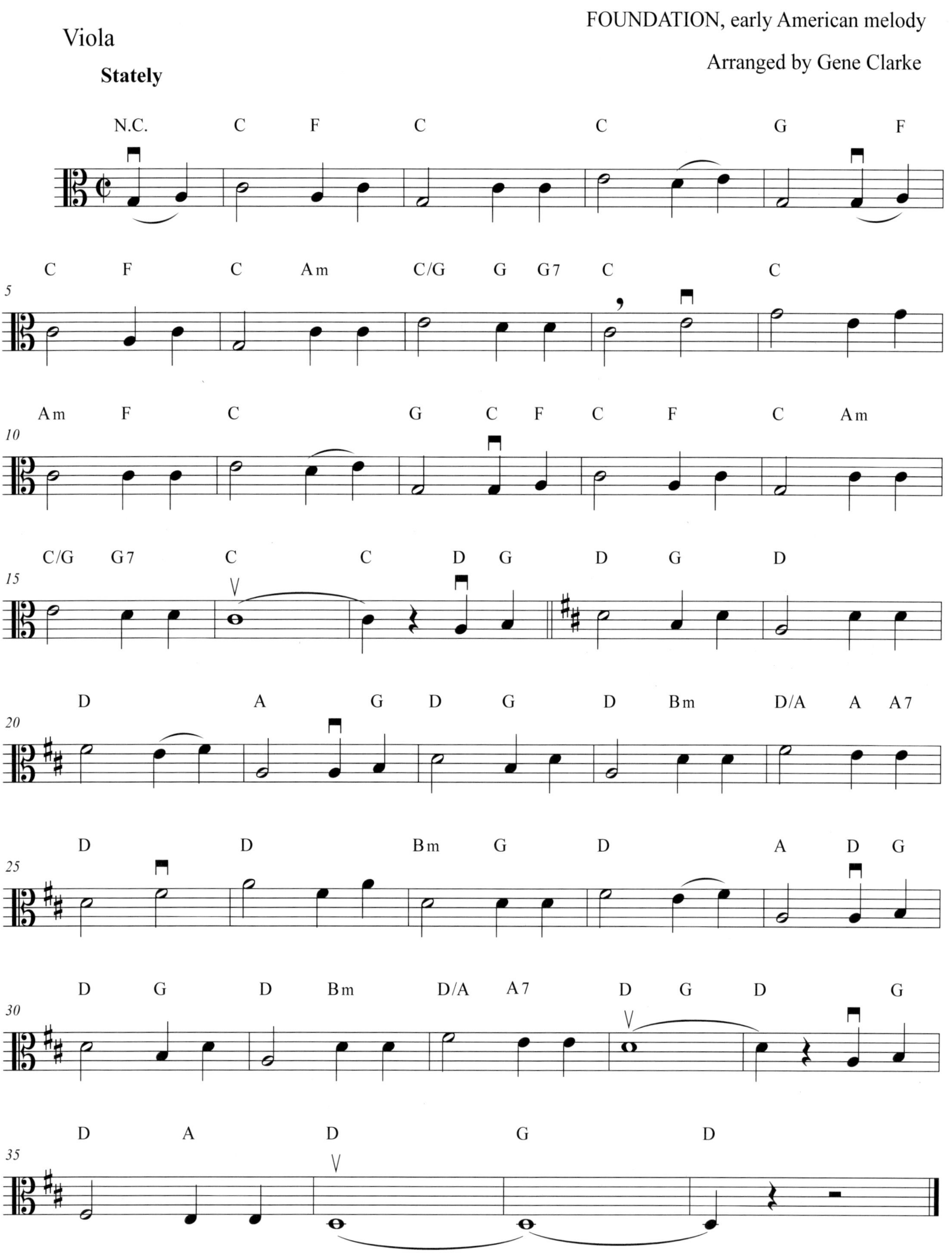

I Need Thee Every Hour

Viola

NEED, by
Robert Lowry, 1873
arranged by Gene Clarke

Slowly

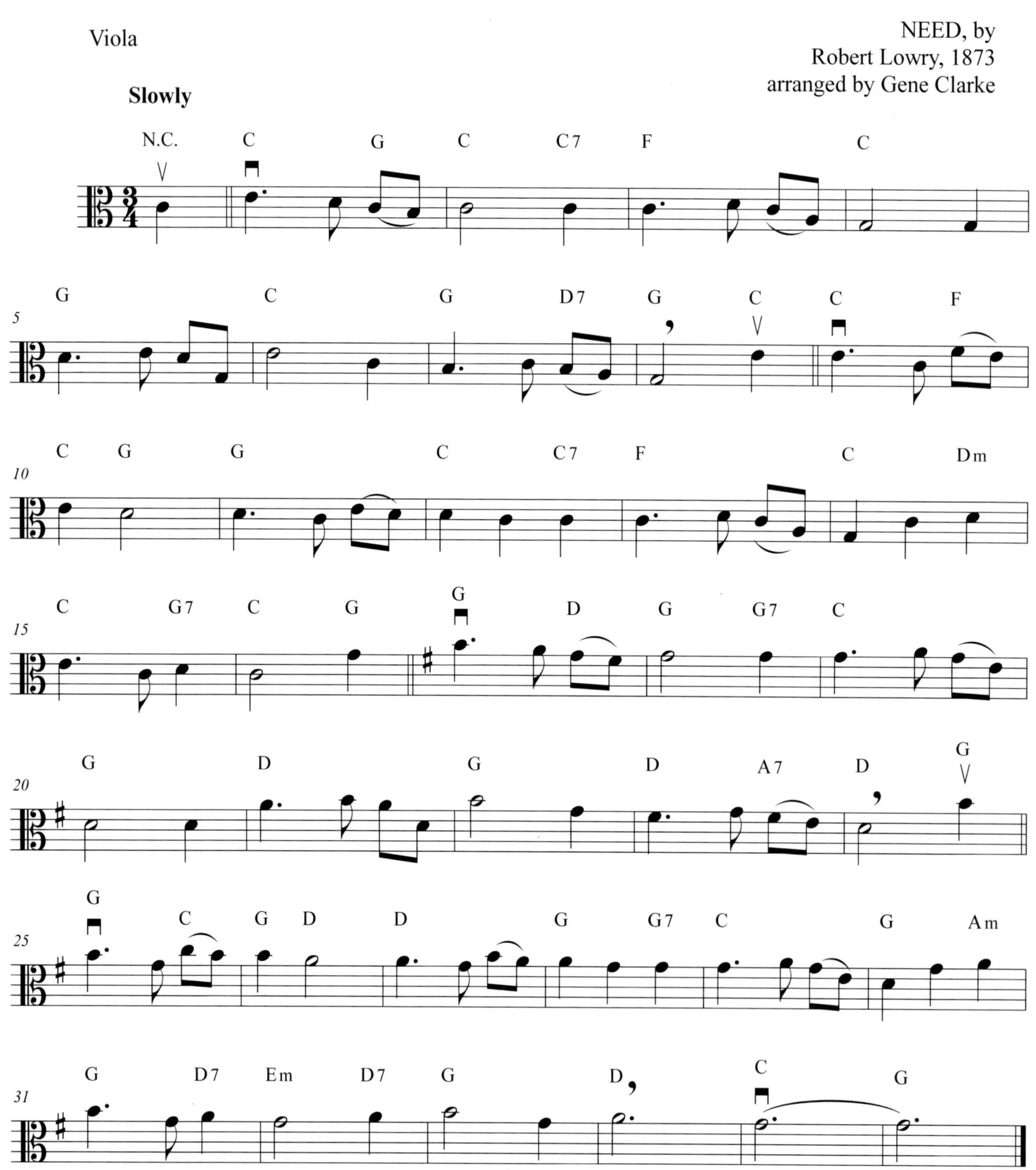

I Surrender All

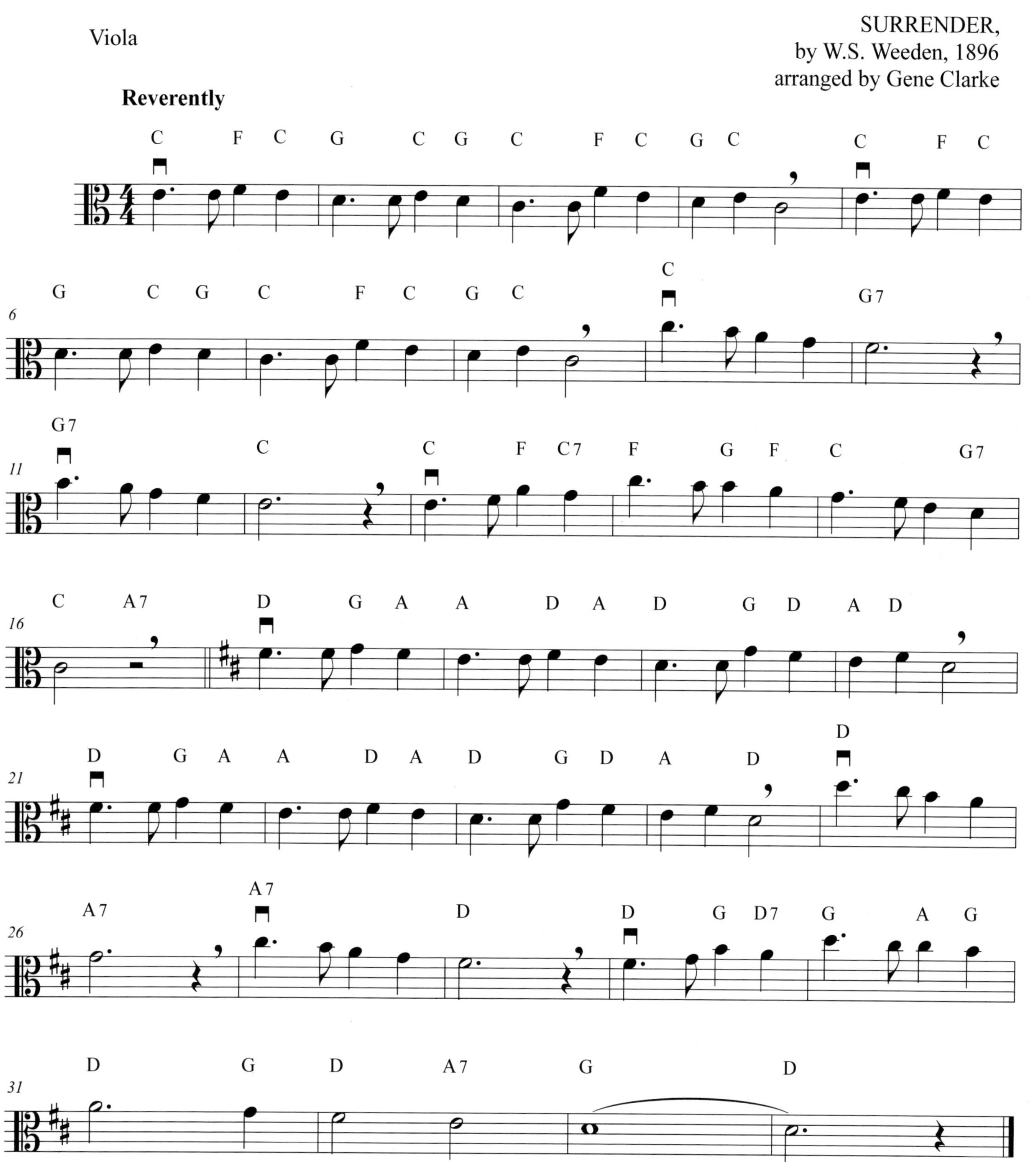

Jesus, Keep Me Near the Cross

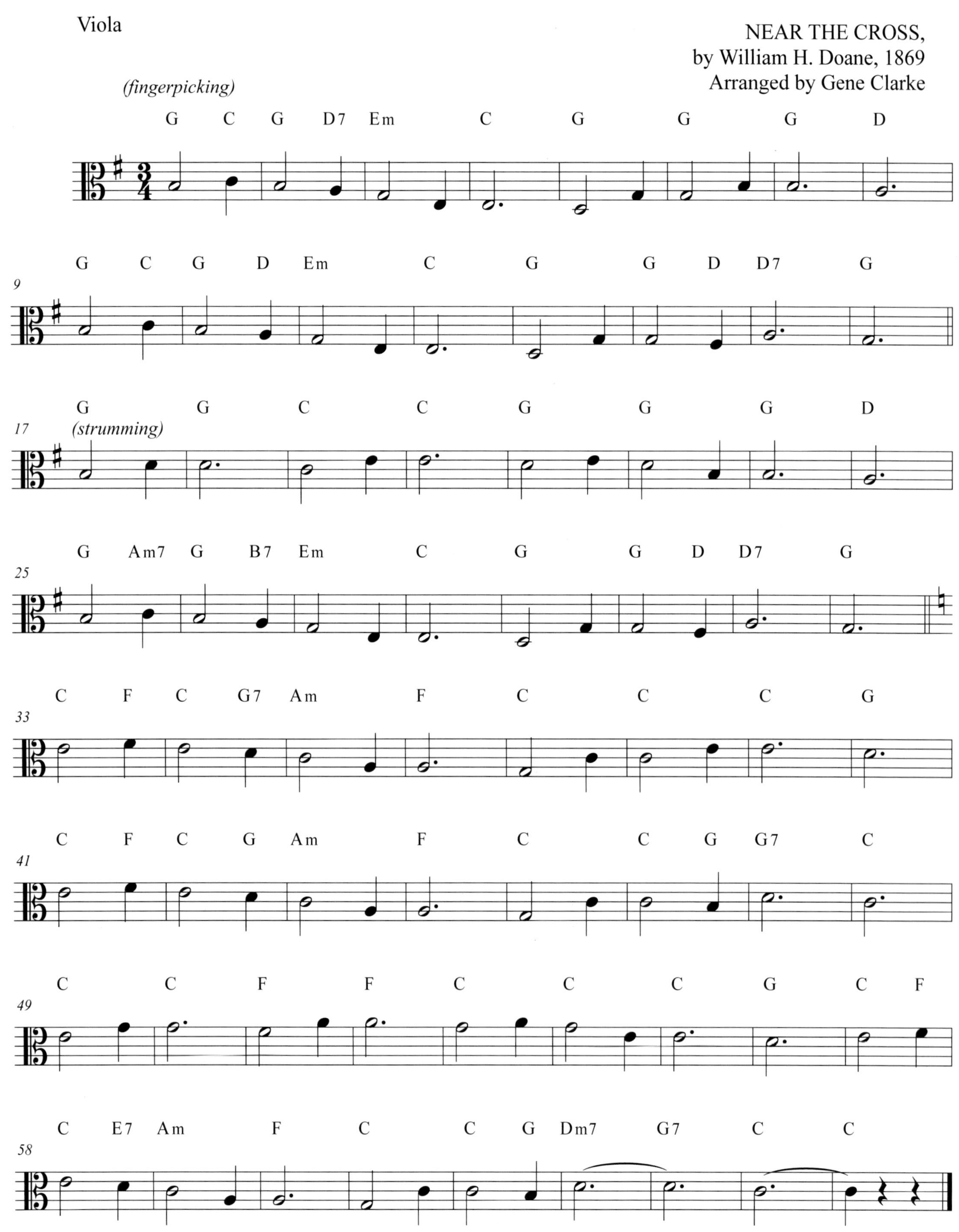

Jesus Loves Me

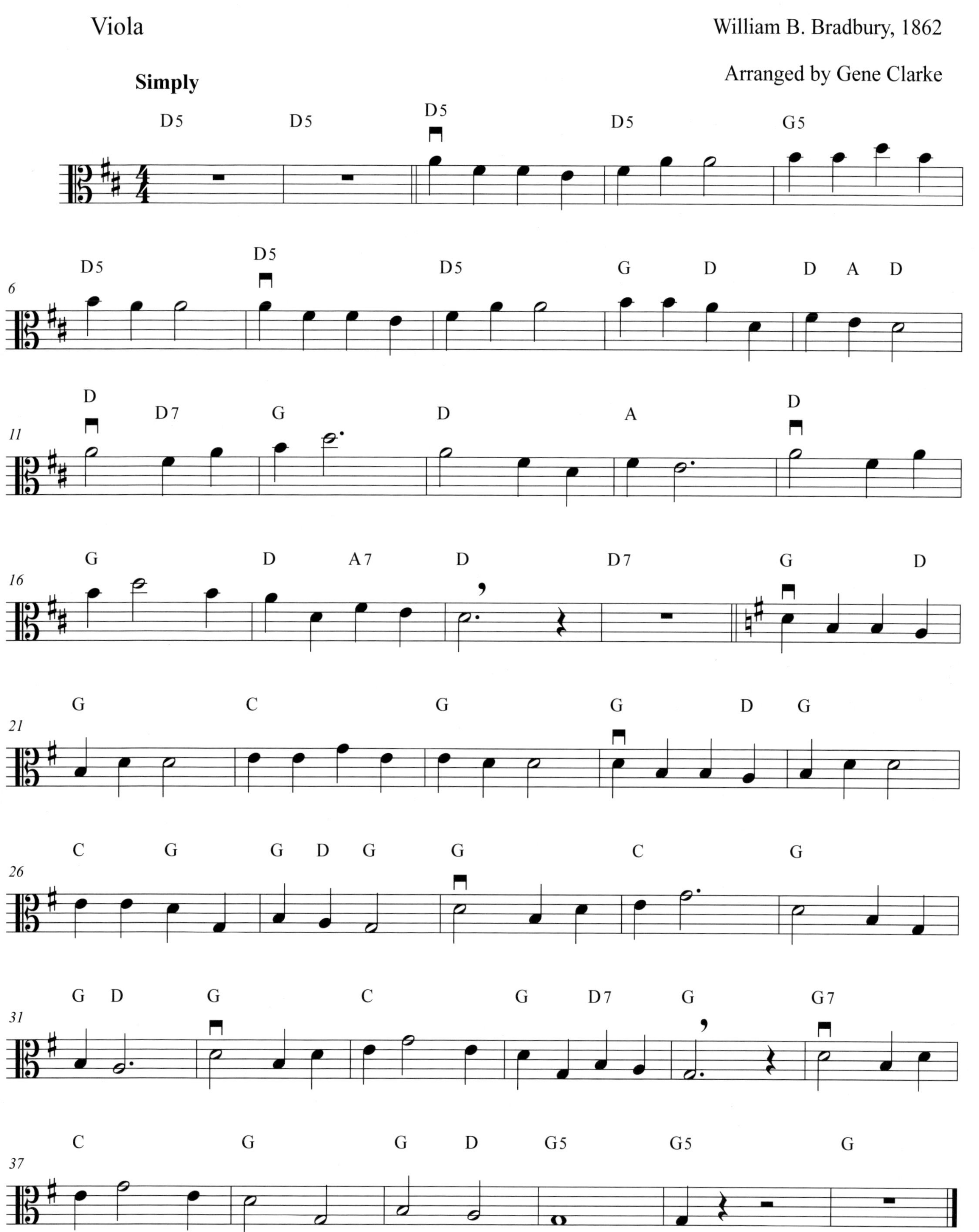

My Faith Looks Up to Thee

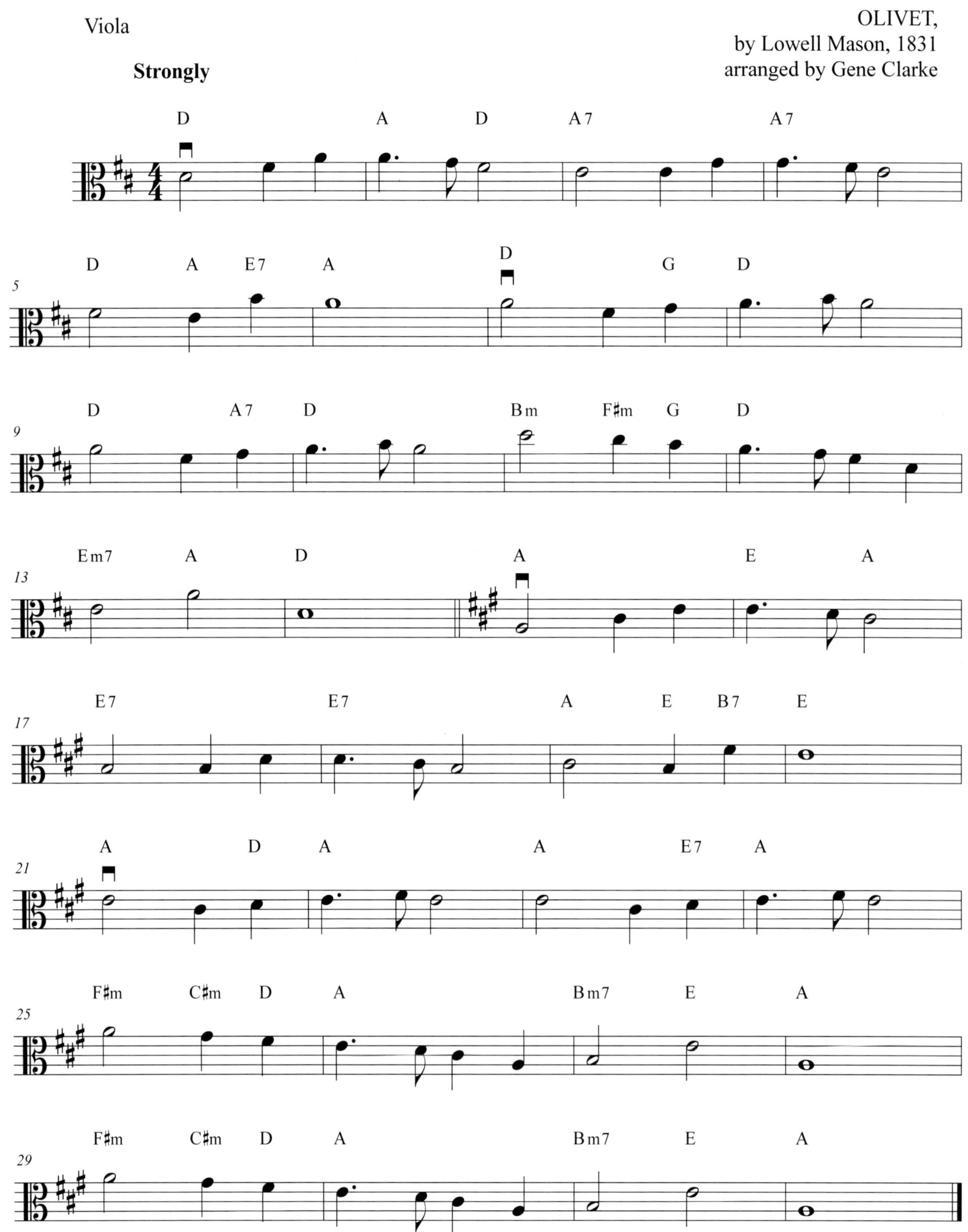

O How I Love Jesus

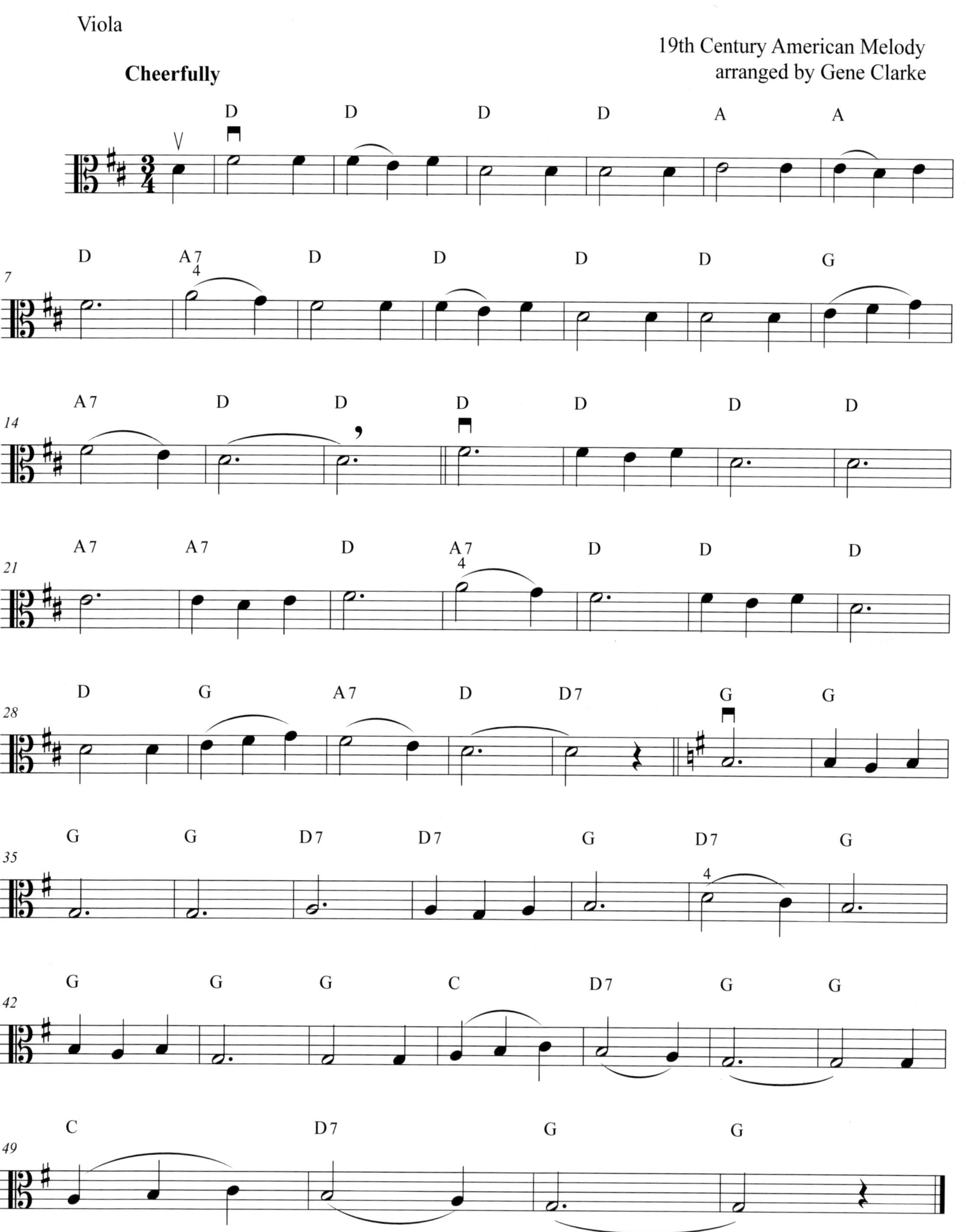

Savior, Like a Shepherd Lead Us

BRADBURY, by
William B. Bradbury, 1859

Arranged by Gene Clarke

Viola

Gently

D A7 D A7 D A7 D A7

6 D A7 D A7 D A7 D D7

11 G D Em A7 D D7 G

16 D Bm Em A7 D D7 G G

21 D7 G D7 G G D7

26 G G7 C G D7 G G7

31 C G D7 Em

35 G Em Am D7 G C G

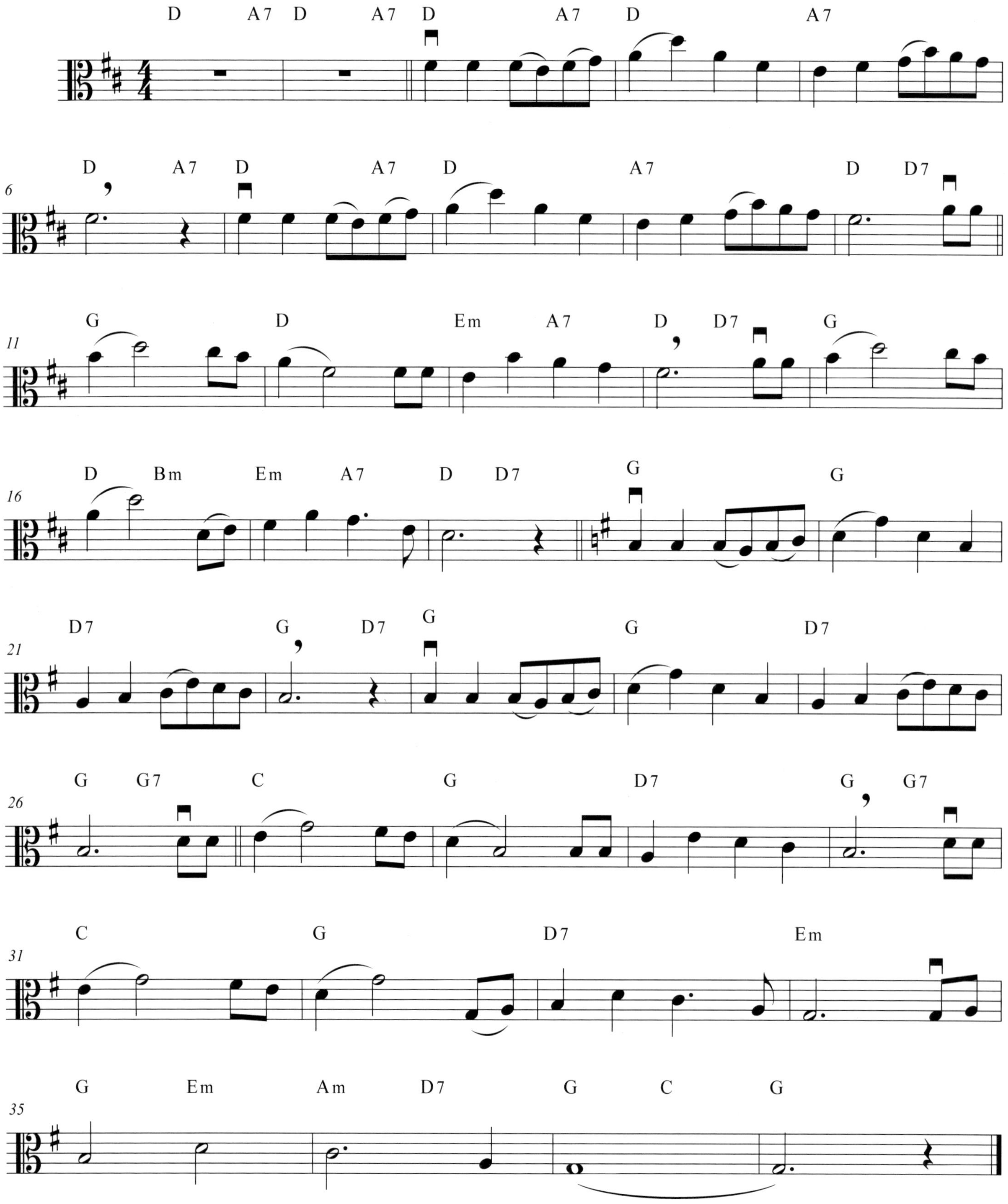

Shall We Gather at the River?

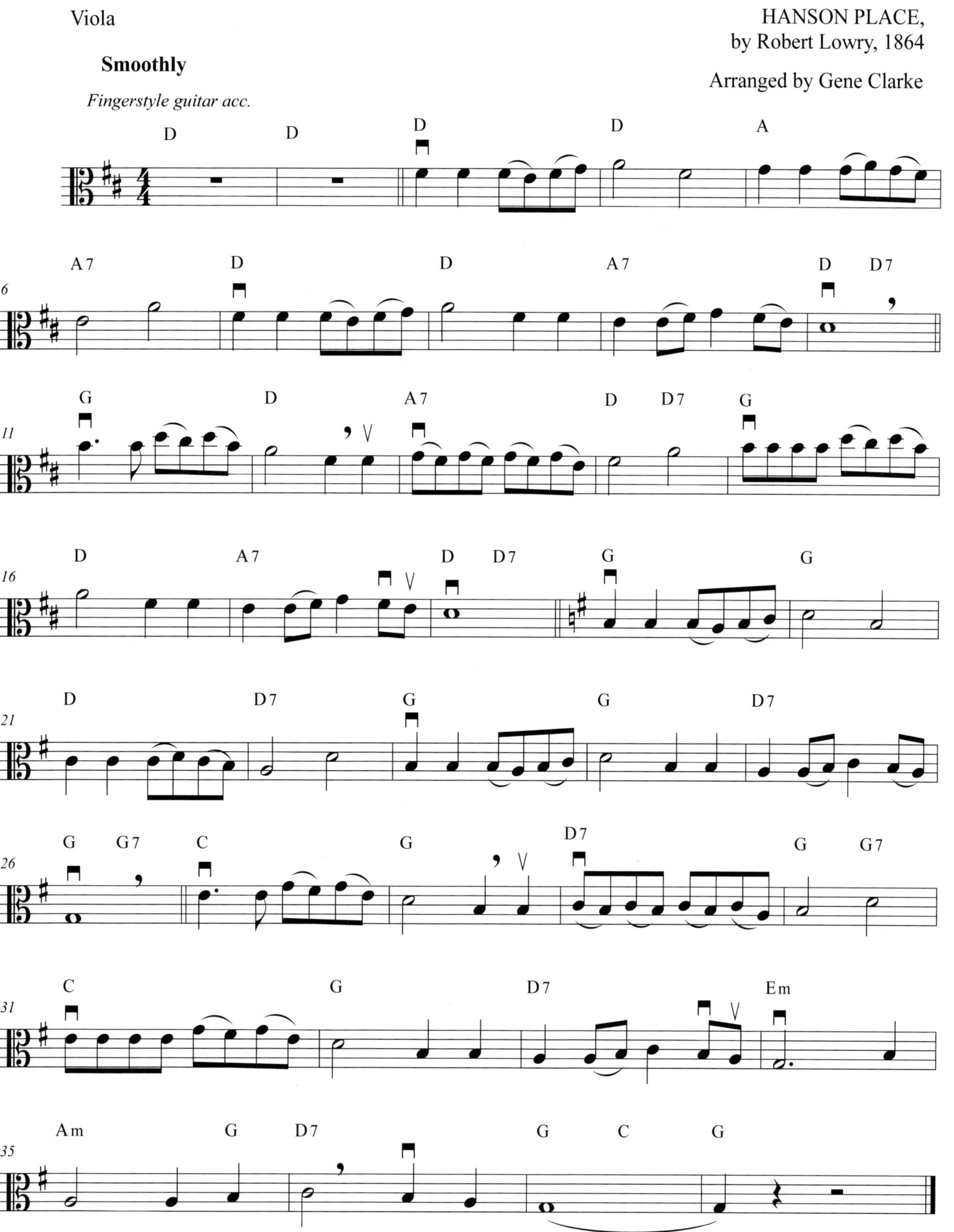

Stand Up, Stand Up for Jesus

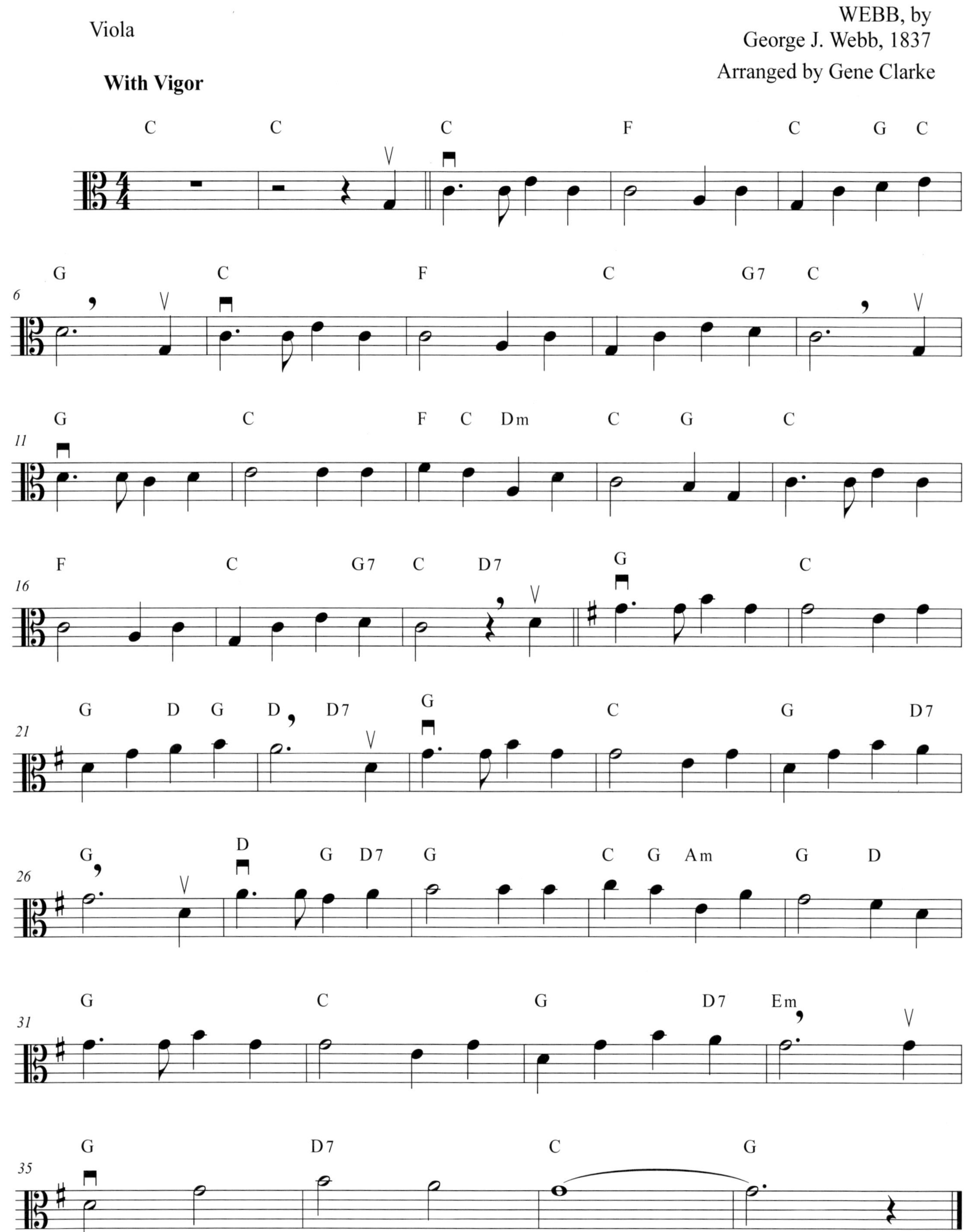

There is a Fountain

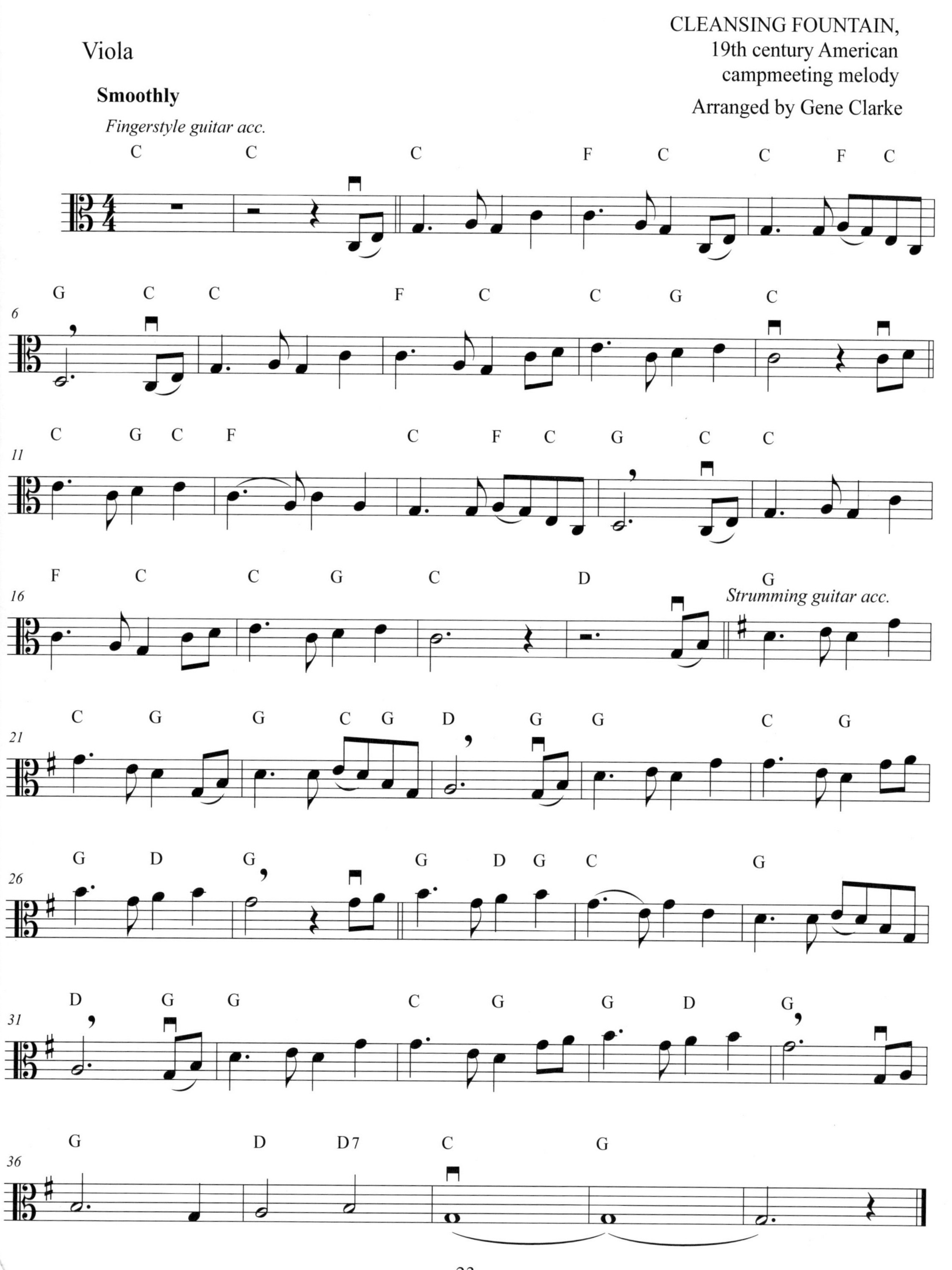

Sweet Hour of Prayer

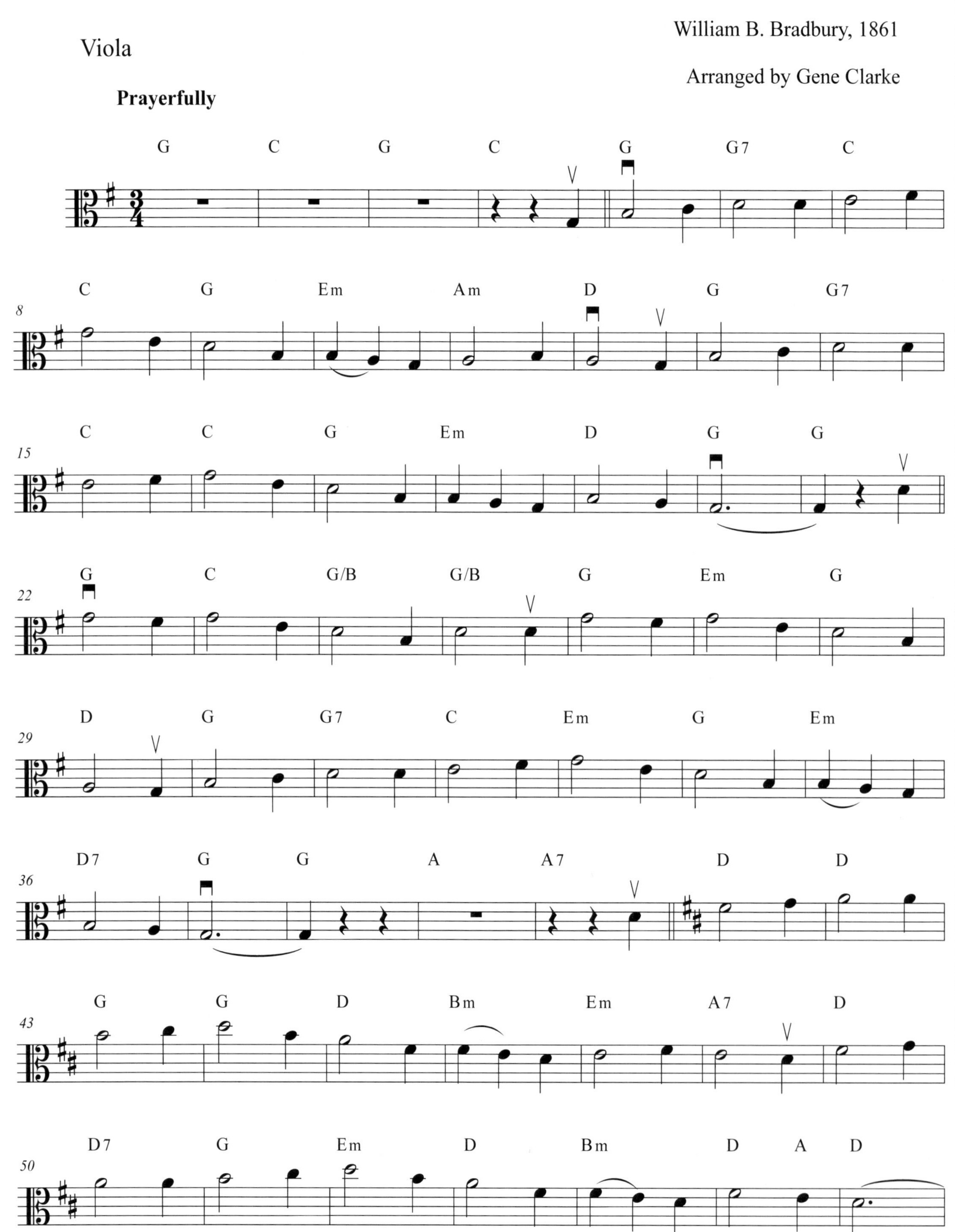

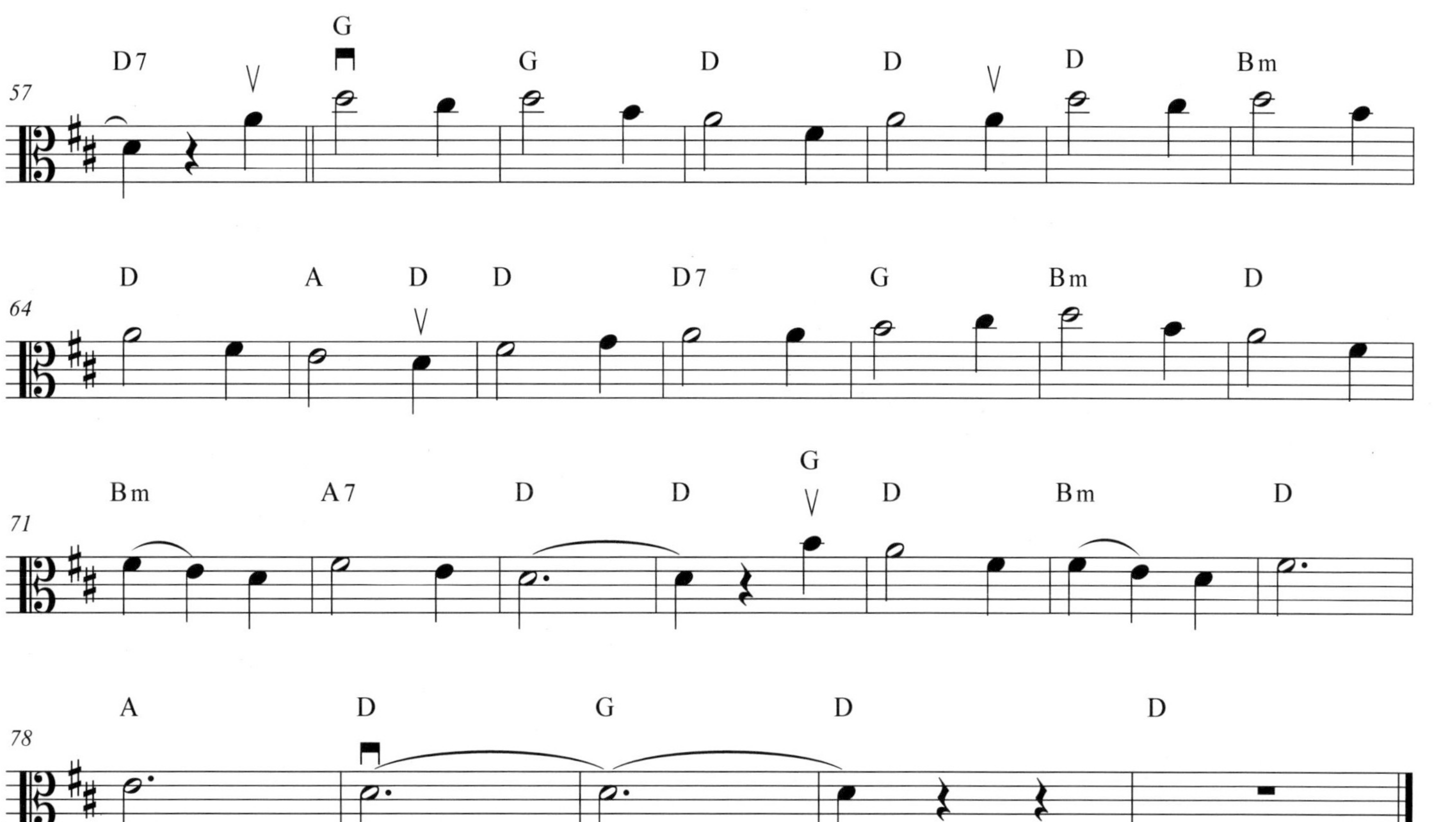
57
D7 G G D D D Bm
64
D A D D D7 G Bm D
71
Bm A7 D D G D Bm D
78
A D G D D

Wonderful Words of Life

Viola

With a Lilt

WORDS OF LIFE,
by Phillip P. Bliss
Arranged by Gene Clarke

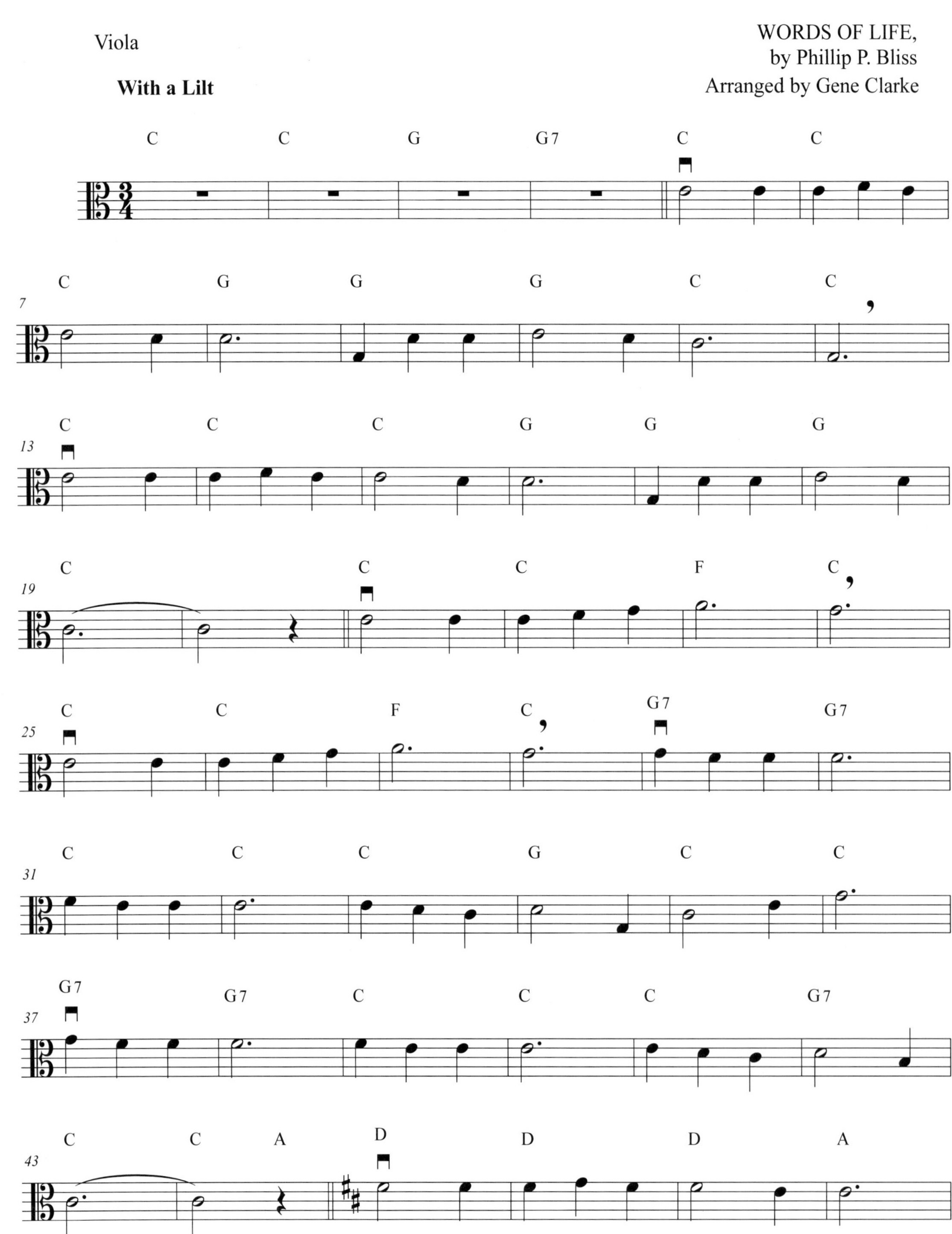

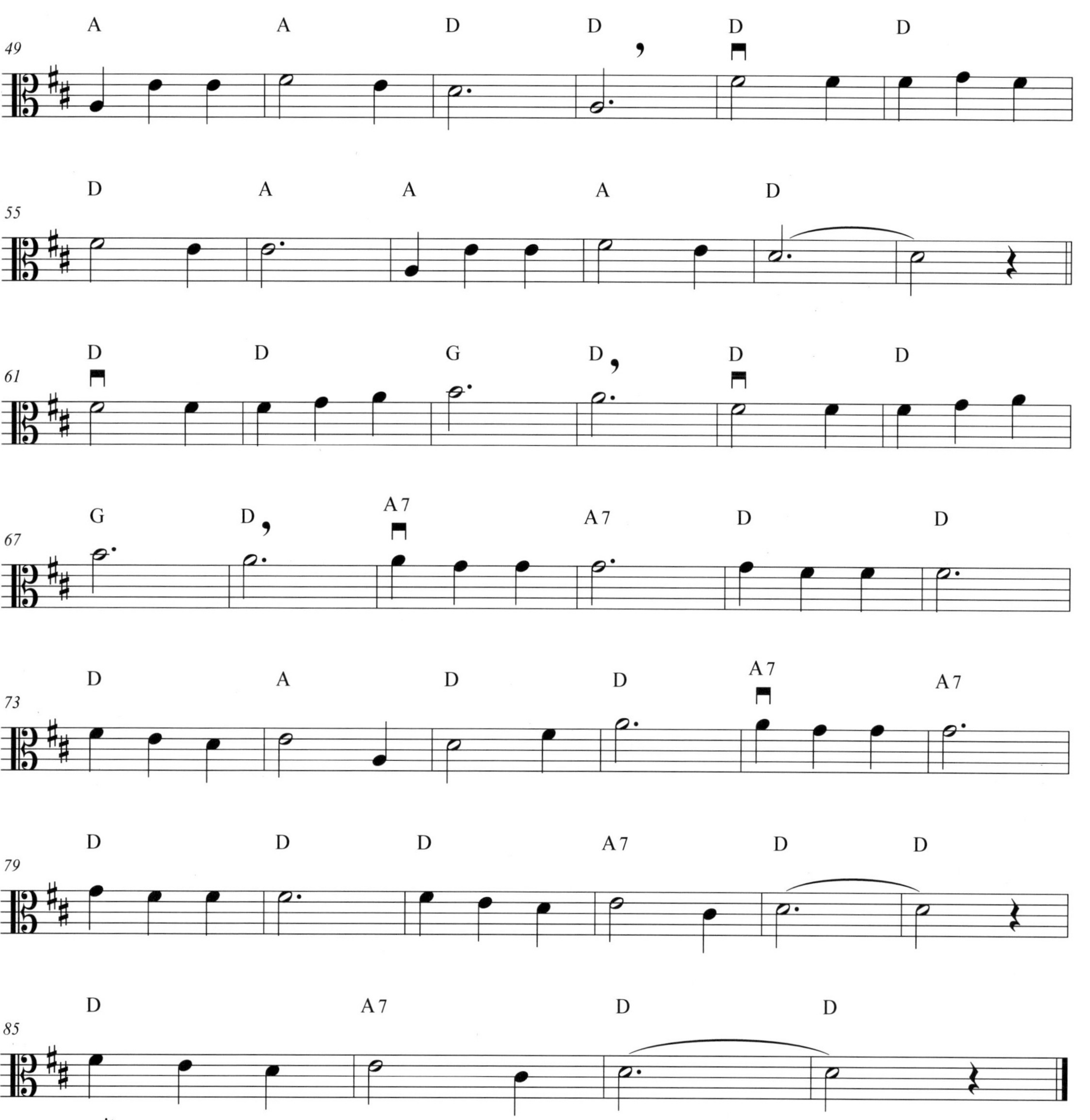
A A D D D D
49
D A A A D
55
D D G D D D
61
G D A 7 A 7 D D
67
D A D D A 7 A 7
73
D D D A 7 D D
79
D A 7 D D
85
rit.

What a Friend We Have in Jesus

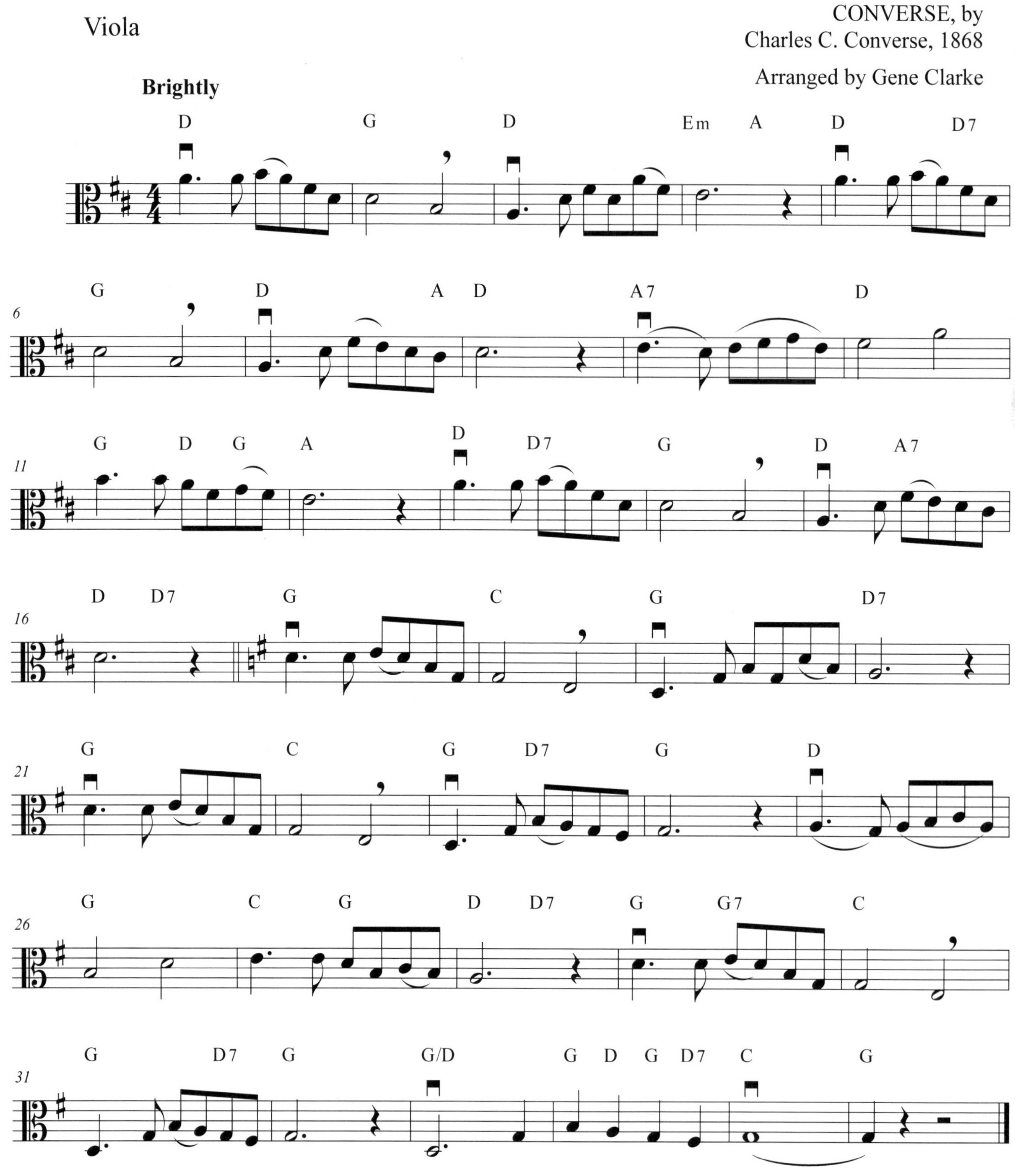